MILES DAVIS

Play-Along

To access online content visit:
www.halleonard.com/mylibrary

Enter Code
3557-7975-8670-7562

ISBN 978-1-4950-7508-7

HAL•LEONARD®
7777 W. BLUEMOUND RD. P.O. BOX 13819 MILWAUKEE, WI 53213

For more information on the Real Book series, including community forums, please visit
www.OfficialRealBook.com

Visit Hal Leonard Online at
www.halleonard.com

Contents

BLUE IN GREEN

(BALLAD)

— MILES DAVIS

C VERSION

AFTER SOLOS, D.C. AL ⊕

BOPLICITY
(BE BOP LIVES)

— MILES DAVIS/GIL EVANS

C VERSION

FOUR

– MILES DAVIS

C VERSION

FINE

AFTER SOLOS, D.C. AL FINE
(PLAY PICKUPS) (TAKE REPEAT)

FREDDIE FREELOADER

- MILES DAVIS

FINE
(TAKE 2ⁿᵈ ENDING ON SOLOS)

Milestones

- MILES DAVIS

C VERSION

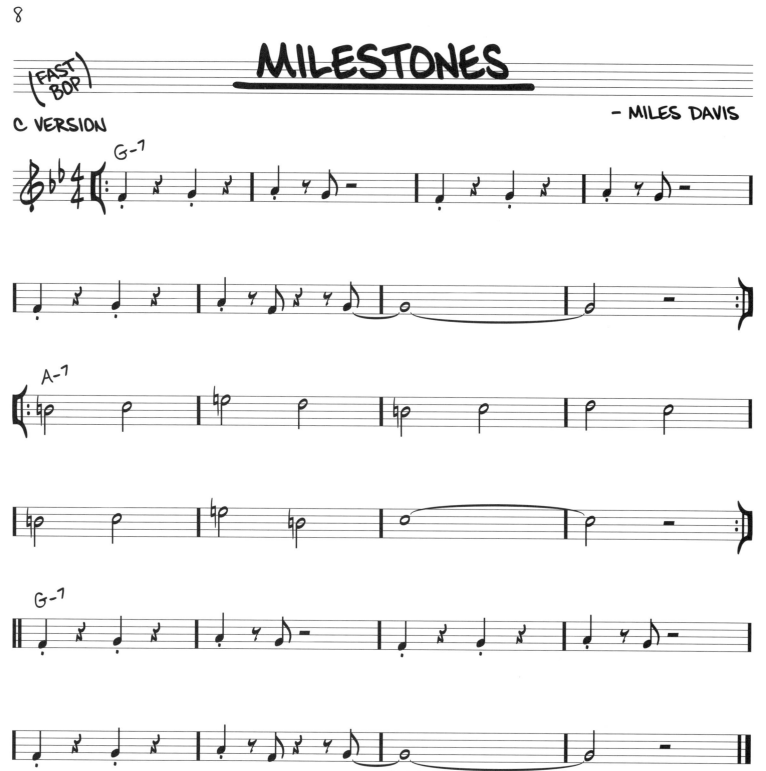

FINE

Nardis

MED. FAST JAZZ

– MILES DAVIS

C VERSION

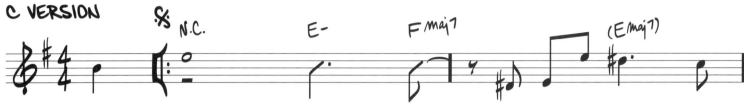

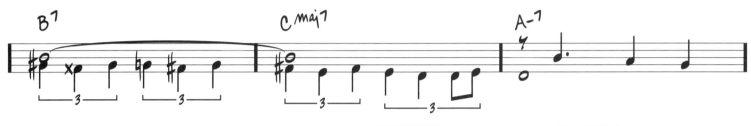

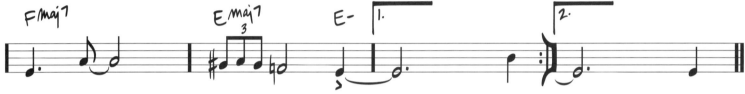

AFTER SOLOS, D.S. AL FINE (PLAY PICKUP)
[NO ANTICIPATIONS ON SOLOS]

SEVEN STEPS TO HEAVEN

— MILES DAVIS/VICTOR FELDMAN

C F¹³   Eb¹³   (3Xs)   F¹³   (SOLO BREAK)----------

D SOLOS

F maj7 | E-7 A7 | D-7 | G7

G-7 | C7 | Ebb Eb | Fb

E C maj7 | D-7 G7 | C maj7 | F-7 Bb7

Eb maj7 | Ab-7 Db7 | Gb maj7 | G-7 C7

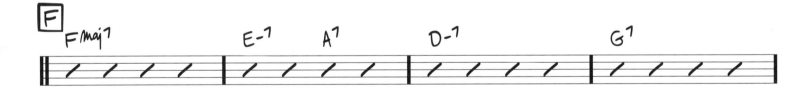

F F maj7 | E-7 A7 | D-7 | G7

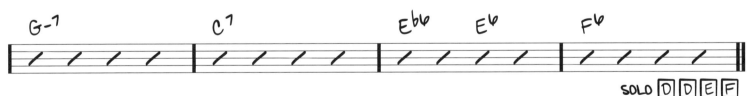

G-7 | C7 | Ebb Eb | Fb

SOLO D D E F
LAST TIME, D.S. AL ⊕

⊕ Ebb Eb Fb N.C. (4Xs) F¹³   Eb¹³   (6Xs) F¹³

SO WHAT

– MILES DAVIS

C VERSION

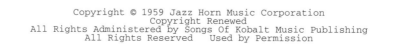

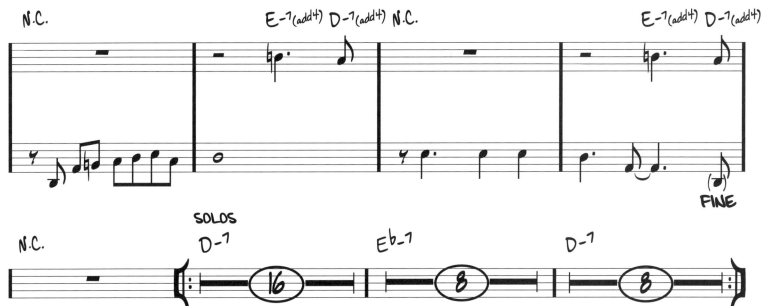

SOLAR

– MILES DAVIS

C VERSION

MED. SWING

REPEAT HEAD IN/OUT

Walkin'

MED. SWING

C VERSION

– RICHARD CARPENTER

SOLO ON F BLUES
AFTER SOLOS, D.S. AL ⊕
(PLAY PICKUPS) (TAKE REPEAT)

BLUE IN GREEN

— MILES DAVIS

B♭ VERSION

(BALLAD)

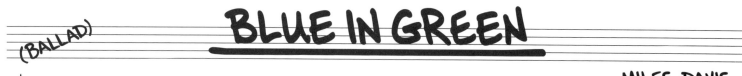

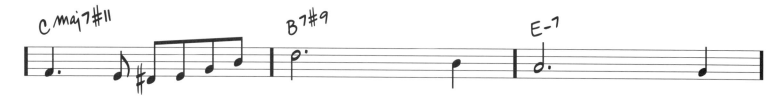

AFTER SOLOS, D.C. AL ⊕

BOPLICITY
(BE BOP LIVES)

— MILES DAVIS/GIL EVANS

Bb VERSION

FOUR

— MILES DAVIS

MED.
(SWING)

B♭ VERSION

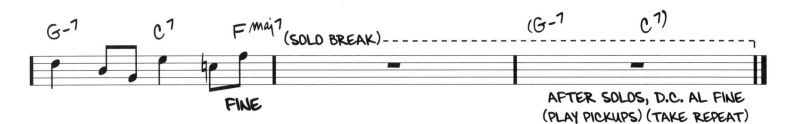

FINE

AFTER SOLOS, D.C. AL FINE
(PLAY PICKUPS) (TAKE REPEAT)

FREDDIE FREELOADER

– MILES DAVIS

FINE
(TAKE 2nd ENDING ON SOLOS.)

Milestones

– Miles Davis

B♭ VERSION

FINE

Nardis

— MILES DAVIS

Bb VERSION

MED. FAST JAZZ

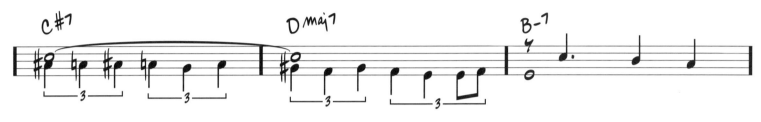

FINE
AFTER SOLOS, D.S. AL FINE (PLAY PICKUP)
[NO ANTICIPATIONS ON SOLOS]

SEVEN STEPS TO HEAVEN

— MILES DAVIS/VICTOR FELDMAN

B♭ VERSION

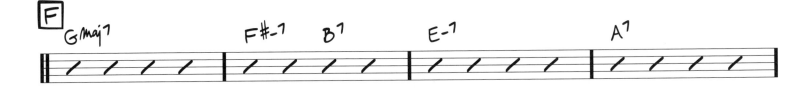

SOLO [D] [D] [E] [F]
LAST TIME, D.S. AL ⊕

SO WHAT

– MILES DAVIS

MED. JAZZ

B♭ VERSION

Solar

– MILES DAVIS

Bb VERSION

MED.
(SWING)

REPEAT HEAD IN/OUT

Walkin'

— RICHARD CARPENTER

B♭ Version

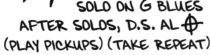

SOLO ON G BLUES
AFTER SOLOS, D.S. AL ⊕
(PLAY PICKUPS) (TAKE REPEAT)

BLUE IN GREEN

BOPLICITY
(BE BOP LIVES)

— MILES DAVIS/GIL EVANS

FOUR

— MILES DAVIS

Eb VERSION

FINE

AFTER SOLOS, D.C. AL FINE
(PLAY PICKUPS) (TAKE REPEAT)

FREDDIE FREELOADER

— MILES DAVIS

(MED. BLUES)

Eb VERSION

FINE
(TAKE 2ⁿᵈ ENDING ON SOLOS)

Milestones

— Miles Davis

Nardis

– MILES DAVIS

Eb Version

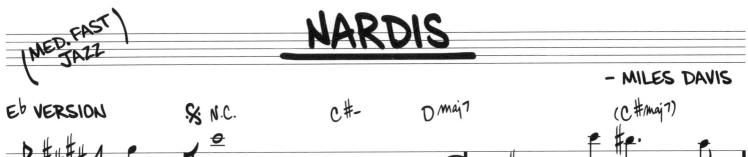

FINE

AFTER SOLOS, D.S. AL FINE (PLAY PICKUP)
[NO ANTICIPATIONS ON SOLOS]

Seven Steps to Heaven

— Miles Davis/Victor Feldman

Eb Version

(Fast Bop)

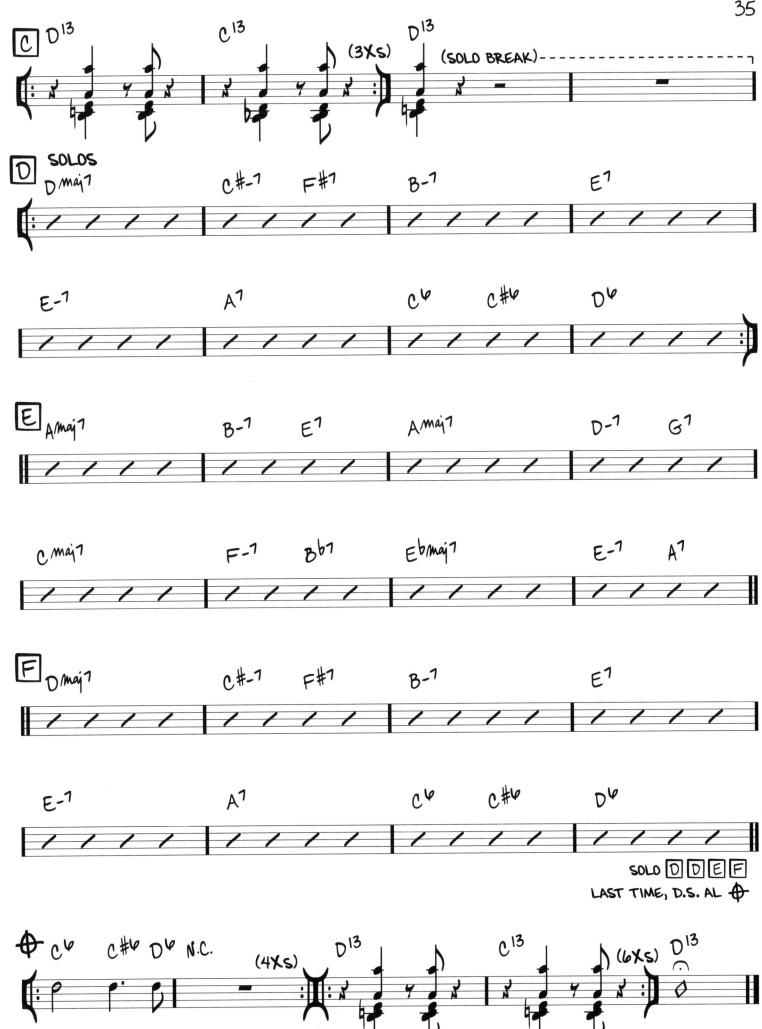

SO WHAT

- MILES DAVIS

Eb VERSION

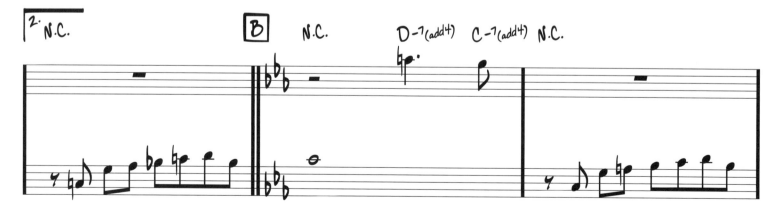

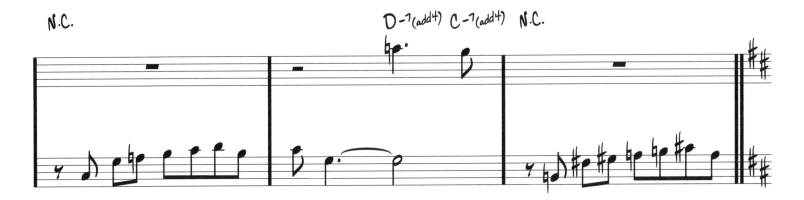

FINE

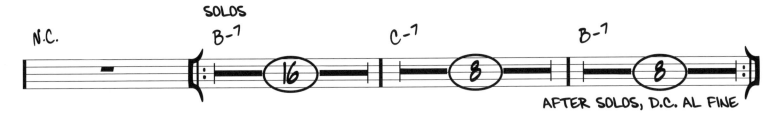

AFTER SOLOS, D.C. AL FINE

Solar

Miles Davis

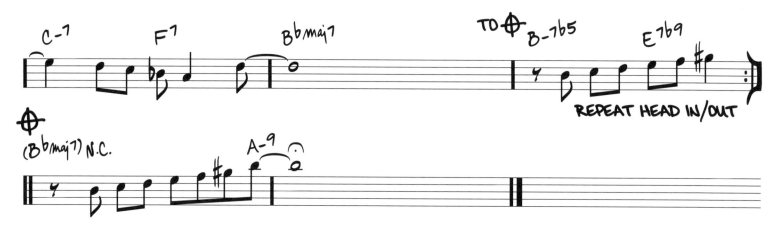

REPEAT HEAD IN/OUT

Walkin'

Eb Version

— RICHARD CARPENTER

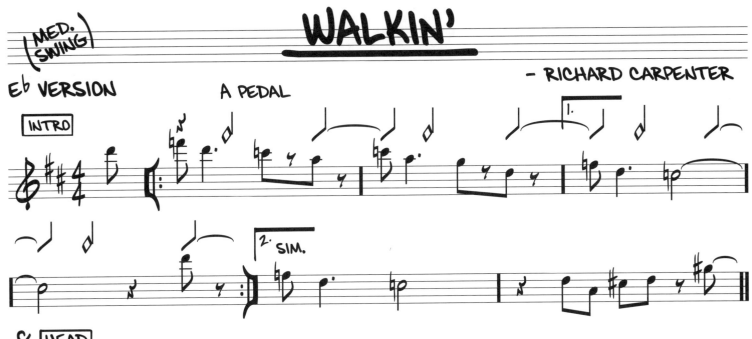

SOLO ON D BLUES
AFTER SOLOS, D.S. AL ⊕
(PLAY PICKUPS) (TAKE REPEAT)

BLUE IN GREEN

— MILES DAVIS

(BALLAD)

C BASS VERSION

AFTER SOLOS, D.C. AL ⊕

BOPLICITY
(BE BOP LIVES)

— MILES DAVIS/GIL EVANS

C BASS VERSION

FINE

FOUR

– MILES DAVIS

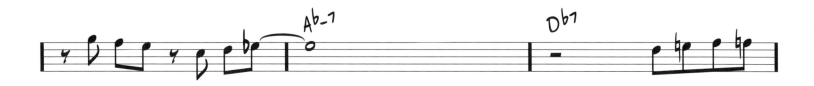

FINE

AFTER SOLOS, D.S. AL FINE
(PLAY PICKUPS) (TAKE REPEAT)

FREDDIE FREELOADER

— MILES DAVIS

(MED. BLUES)

C BASS VERSION

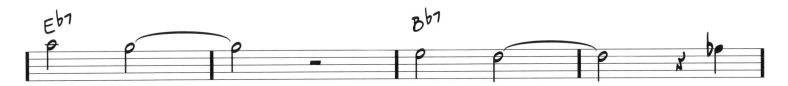

FINE
(TAKE 2ⁿᵈ ENDING ON SOLOS)

Milestones

- Miles Davis

C BASS VERSION

FINE

Nardis

— MILES DAVIS

MED. FAST JAZZ

C BASS VERSION

FINE

AFTER SOLOS, D.S. AL FINE (PLAY PICKUP)
[NO ANTICIPATIONS ON SOLOS]

Seven Steps to Heaven

— Miles Davis/Victor Feldman

C BASS VERSION

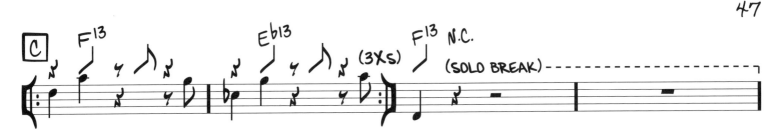

C F¹³ Eᵇ¹³ (3Xs) F¹³ N.C. (SOLO BREAK)- - - - - - - - - - - - - - -

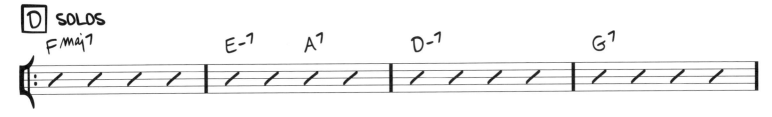

D SOLOS
Fmaj7 | E-7 A7 | D-7 | G7

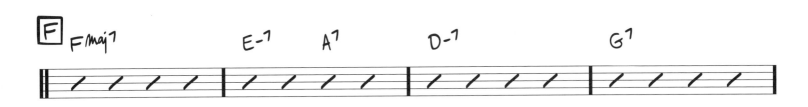

G-7 | C7 | Eᵇᵇ Eᵇ | Fᵇ

E Cmaj7 | D-7 G7 | Cmaj7 | F-7 Bᵇ7

Eᵇmaj7 | Aᵇ-7 Dᵇ7 | Gᵇmaj7 | G-7 C7

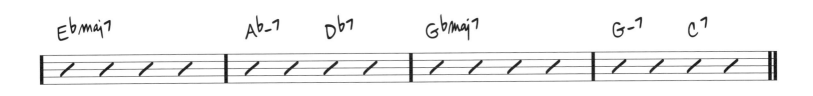

F Fmaj7 | E-7 A7 | D-7 | G7

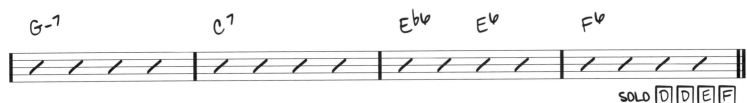

G-7 | C7 | Eᵇᵇ Eᵇ | Fᵇ

SOLO D D E F
LAST TIME, D.S. AL ⊕

⊕ Eᵇᵇ Eᵇ Fᵇ N.C. (4Xs) F¹³ Eᵇ¹³ (6Xs) F¹³

SO WHAT

— MILES DAVIS

C BASS VERSION

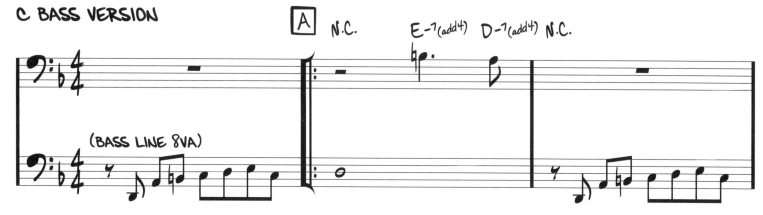

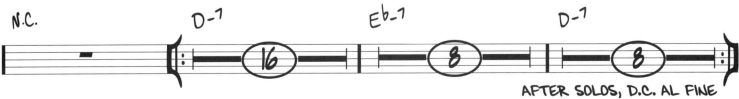

AFTER SOLOS, D.C. AL FINE

SOLAR

— MILES DAVIS

C BASS VERSION

(MED. SWING)

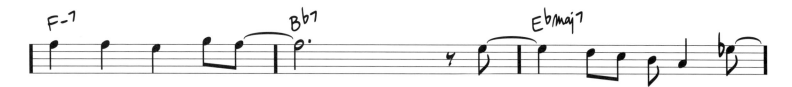

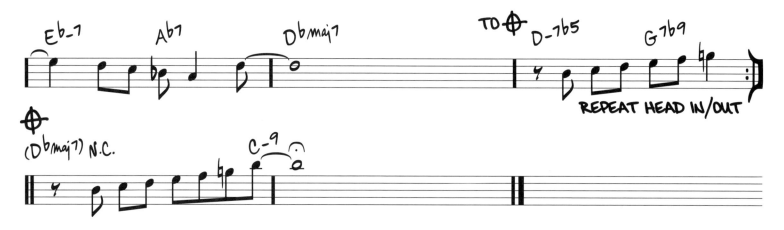

REPEAT HEAD IN/OUT

WALKIN'

C BASS VERSION

— RICHARD CARPENTER

SOLO ON F BLUES
AFTER SOLOS, D.S. AL ⊕
(PLAY PICKUPS) (TAKE REPEAT)

THE REAL BOOK MULTI-TRACKS

MAIDEN VOYAGE Play-Along

MILES DAVIS Play-Along

ALL BLUES Play-Along

CHARLIE PARKER Play-Along

JAZZ FUNK Play-Along

THE REAL BOOK MULTI-TRACKS

TODAY'S BEST WAY TO PRACTICE JAZZ!

Accurate, easy-to-read lead sheets and professional, customizable audio tracks accessed online for 10 songs.

1. MAIDEN VOYAGE PLAY-ALONG

Autumn Leaves • Blue Bossa • Doxy • Footprints • Maiden Voyage • Now's the Time • On Green Dolphin Street • Satin Doll • Summertime • Tune Up.
00196616 Book with Online Media $17.99

2. MILES DAVIS PLAY-ALONG

Blue in Green • Boplicity (Be Bop Lives) • Four • Freddie Freeloader • Milestones • Nardis • Seven Steps to Heaven • So What • Solar • Walkin'.
00196798 Book with Online Media $17.99

3. ALL BLUES PLAY-ALONG

All Blues • Back at the Chicken Shack • Billie's Bounce (Bill's Bounce) • Birk's Works • Blues by Five • C-Jam Blues • Mr. P.C. • One for Daddy-O • Reunion Blues • Turnaround.
00196692 Book with Online Media $17.99

4. CHARLIE PARKER PLAY-ALONG

Anthropology • Blues for Alice • Confirmation • Donna Lee • K.C. Blues • Moose the Mooche • My Little Suede Shoes • Ornithology • Scrapple from the Apple • Yardbird Suite.
00196799 Book with Online Media $17.99

5. JAZZ FUNK PLAY-ALONG

Alligator Bogaloo • The Chicken • Cissy Strut • Cold Duck Time • Comin' Home Baby • Mercy, Mercy, Mercy • Put It Where You Want It • Sidewinder • Tom Cat • Watermelon Man.
00196728 Book with Online Media $17.99

The interactive, online audio interface includes:
- tempo control
- looping
- buttons to turn each instrument on or off
- lead sheet with follow-along marker
- melody performed by a saxophone or trumpet on the "head in" and "head out."

The full stereo tracks can also be downloaded and played off-line. Separate lead sheets are included for C, B-flat, E-flat and Bass Clef instruments.

HAL•LEONARD®
www.halleonard.com

Prices, content and availability subject to change without notice.

THE REAL BOOK MULTI-TRACKS
Play-Along